Is It a Garden?

by Zoë Clarke

illustrated by Mackinzie Rekers

Is It a Garden?

This garden has no soil.

Not all gardens need mowing.

This garden has a carpet of moss.

Bog Gardens

All bog gardens are damp.

Look at this garden!
Plants can grow big and strong.

On the Roof

This garden is little.
It grows on the roof of some bins.

This roof garden has lots of sun.

Street Gardens

It can get hot.
Trees keep roads cool.

Some plants grow up high.

Have Fun!

This garden is growing in a car!

You can trim plants.

Grow a Garden

Put soil into cans.
Sow seeds in the soil.

Pack seedlings into worn out boots.

You can have a herb path.
Fill cracks in the path with seeds.

Do not mow
and things
will grow!

wet

fun

roof

high

Encourage students to read the words and match them to the pictures.